OLD NEGATIVES

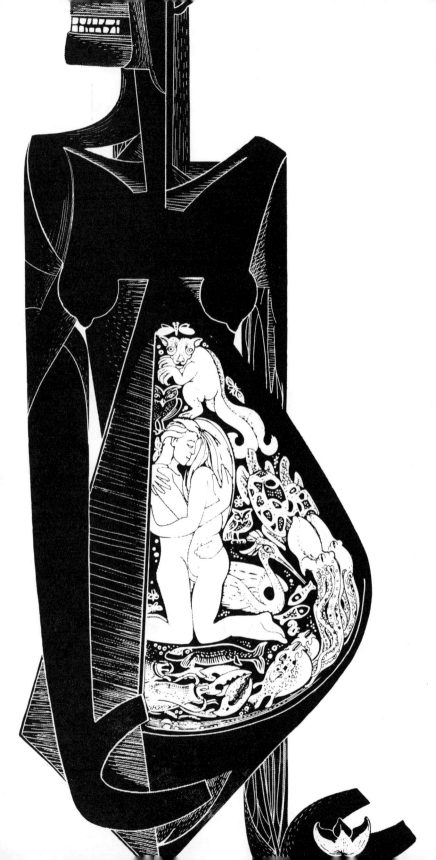

OLD NEGATIVES

four verse sequences
by Alasdair Gray

1 9 8 9

JONATHAN CAPE
32 BEDFORD SQUARE

LINES REVIEW published the verses here called Unfit in the winter of 1962–63, those called Vacancy in the summer of 1963; GLASGOW UNIVERSITY MAGAZINE published To Andrew, Before One in March 1971; THE GLASGOW REVIEW Not Striving in the summer of 1972; the Strathclyde University poetry magazine STRATA published Cowardly, Lost Absence and The Thinker in their winter–spring number of 1984; the Scottish broadsheet CLANJAMFRIE published Cowardly about the same time; CHAPMAN magazine published the whole 1952–57 sequence in its fiftieth edition, winter of 1987; PROSPICE the 1957–61 sequence in the summer of 1988; the GLASGOW HERALD and BÊTE NOIR the 1961–71 sequence in the autumn of 1988.

The illustrations on the jacket of the hardback edition and on pages 2, 9 and 29 are from a set made in 1969–71 with help from a Scottish Arts Council grant, and are reproduced by permission of Glasgow Hunterian Museum.

The above verses, with others, are here published in their final and correctly named forms, in the spring of 1989 by JONATHAN CAPE LTD,
32 BEDFORD SQUARE, LONDON WC1B 3SG

TYPESET BY SELECTMOVE LTD, LONDON
PRINTED IN GREAT BRITAIN BY
BUTLER & TANNER LTD, FROME AND LONDON

A CIP CATALOGUE RECORD FOR THIS BOOK IS AVAILABLE FROM THE BRITISH LIBRARY
ISBN 0–224–02304–7
0–224–02656–9 (pbk)

Amy
Fleming
11·1·1902
24·5·1952

TABLE OF

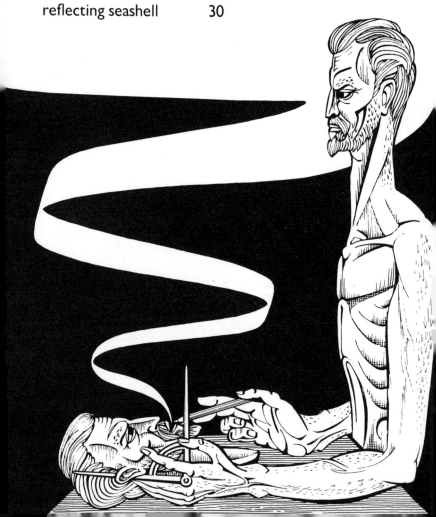

CONTENTS

IN A
COLD
ROOM
1952–57

We came through a dark arch to a sky of moon,
to a wooden stair and broken house
black against blue luminous night air
and inside two dim rooms we stamped our feet
to saxophone and candlelight and drum-beat
late into the night.

And now the clock's tick tells me that I suck the dregs
of one more idle day,
and here I sit and watch the inchlong candlewick.
One at a time my friends all move away
to crouch within the dint of mattress and of couch,
and still I wait that hint of revelation late hours bring
though what they will reveal I cannot say.

What is there for me when the morning comes?
A kitten scrabbling cold gnawed rabbit bones
among the tinkling cinders of a hearth,
desolate wisdom got avoiding the known good,
a tramcar moaning down an empty street,
a memory that fingers old regrets.
Few thoughts. No purpose. A remote hope,
for when these couples find they cannot sleep
a girl I know will yawn and rub her eyes,
untwist her soft hair from her lover's beard
and dress herself, and rise
perhaps to wash her face and brew some tea,
perhaps to talk with me.

From the soul's proper loneliness love and affection seem
part substance and part dream
held in the mouth in the same way the snake carries its eggs
if gripped too hard they break,
leaving a few grains of dust
and a heart crippled by its weight of lust.

Let me be honest and condemn my love
because of what it does not make in me,
not out of wounded vanity and pride
but for the nothing that it leaves inside.

If love was the dream of a stream and bed a boat
how sweet to float with you my dear
down through the meadows of flowering rush
to the hush hush of breath
over the weir of death.

But love is not just knowledge and tenderness,
a sympathy of brain and heart,
it must be felt hard in the lower part.
Rotten with sympathy, love is a mistake between us two
because you make as little heat in me
as I can make in you.

When will these couples find they cannot sleep?

When the moon sinks and the cat mews for its milk.
When the pressed nostril is sated with coupled skin.

Good. That leaves time for a small experiment:
THE UNION OF TWO VOIDS IN A COLD ROOM.

Observe this unit, gentlemen, which
(for want of a better word)
I call a *self*.
It consists of an envelope enclosed by a void
and enclosing a void
and lined inside and out with nothing but eyes
most of which are shut.
Note that the void enclosing the self
also encloses many other selves
each enclosing a void of its own, which
(in order to differentiate) I call an *abyss*.

Selves can be split into two kinds: solitary and binary.
The self under consideration is solitary.
They can be split into two other kinds: erratic and static.
The self under consideration is erratic.
Why?
Gentlemen,
the enclosed abyss feels threatened by the enclosing void,
thus since its genesis our self has attempted union
with a succession of markedly static selves
in an attempt to join its abyss to theirs
by turning binary.
On every occasion it has failed to achieve collision
through clever footwork on the part of the static selves
(who were never quite as static as they seemed);
also because our self is so erratic
that its trajectory is usually wide of the remark;
also because our self tends to switch
into another field of attraction
                              the moment before collision.
(Collisions can be painful.)

Observe it enter the magnetic field
of a markedly static self, which
(for want of a better word)
I call Veronica.
Aha! This time collision appears inevitable.
It circles her for five or six weeks
gauging her position with reference to other selves,
and the size of her abyss with reference to its own.
Now, taking careful aim,
it starts to travel inward in a spiral accelerating rapidly until
look out! Wham! It's struck her! They're together!
No they're not.
Veronica sidestepped at the last moment.
They merely grazed each other and now her negative attraction
has been switched into positive repulsion
and our self is hurtling into the void behind her.

Did you see what happened at the moment of contact?
Most of the eyes opened for an instant and look!
The place where they touched has split into a mouth.
If we listen carefully perhaps we will hear
the shrill whistle of escaping words.

IN THE BEGINNING WAS THE CAVITY:
EYESOCKET IN NO SKULL, WOUND IN NO FLESH,
THE FACELESS MOUTH, THE COATLESS POCKET.

THIS GOT SUCH HORROR OF ITS OWN VACUITY
IT TRIED AT LENGTH TO SCREAM,
                                AS WHO WOULD NOT?

THEN, AFTER AEONS FIGHTING VOICELESSNESS,
IT SCREAMED A NEBULA OF HYDROGEN.

ODD THAT THE JEWS SHOULD SO
                                HAVE MISCONSTRUED
THAT SCREAM A WORD, THAT CAVITY A GOD.

THEN LIFE APPEARED, A CANCER OF THE CLAY:
SOME MOLECULES CHANCE SHUFFLED
                                        INTO SENSE
WHICH WRIGGLED OUT INTO THE LIGHT OF DAY:
A KNOT OF FIBRE TWITCHING IN THE FIRMAMENT
WITH NO PROVISION FOR ITS GOVERNMENT.

MIND IS A SKY-MACHINE
      KEPT STABLE BY THE BREEZE OF BREATH:
A RACKETY SLIPSHOD THING OF GUT AND NERVE,
PATCHED TUBE AND TWISTED CABLE.
THE ENGINES OF THE HEART AND LUNG SUSTAIN
ITS WINGS ABOVE THE BASEMENT OF A VOID.
BOXED IN ITS SKULL,
    BRAIN IS THE ANEROID BY WHICH WE GAUGE
A LEVEL THROUGH THE PRESSURE OF OUR PAIN
AND STRUGGLE HARD FOR SOME
DEGREE OF STABLE EQUILIBRIUM.

CORRUPTION IS THE ROMAN WHORE TO WHOM
HANGMEN AND POLITICIANS PLAY THE PIMP.
SHE SUCKS ALL SEMEN BACK INTO HER WOMB
AND ISSUES FROM THE PASTURE OF HER THIGHS
BASTARDS WHO MOMENTLY REPOPULATE
THE OCEANS, ROCKS AND SKIES.
THE COFFIN IS NO MORE
THAN BAWDY HOUSE FOR THAT
                    GRAND ROMAN WHORE.

JUST AS THE SUN
  IS ONE SPARK
    IN A TREMENDOUS DARK

SO LOVE IS A POINT OF HEAT IN THAT COLD
  FELT BY THE YOUNG AND
                          VERY OLD WHO KNOW
    ALL FOOTPRINTS MUST BE
                      BLOTTED OUT BY SNOW

AND OUT OF LOVE WE SIT
  WITH HUNGER GNAWING AT OUR WIT
    AND EARS COCKED FOR THE BARK
      OF MOUTHING ANARCHY CROUCHED
              BEASTWISE IN THE DARK

ALONE ALONE COLD COLD COLD AND ALONE
  INSIDE THE BLACK VAST
    ETERNALLY REVOLVING,
     REMORSELESS ENGINE OF THE WHOLE.

MOTHER, LOST MOTHER,
        WHERE HAVE YOU TAKEN ALL MY HEAT
LEAVING ME ALONE,
AS COLD AS WATER, AS COLD AS STONE?

I DID NOT WEEP WHEN YOU DIED,
                I WAS WARM THEN.
WE LAY ON ONE BED,
ONE PILLOW UNDER OUR HEAD.

MOTHER, WHEN I WAS DRIVEN
           OUT OF YOUR QUILTED WOMB
DID YOU MEAN ME TO GO WITH SO LITTLE HEAT
INTO THIS IMPLACABLE MACHINE?

GOD IS A BLEAK FACT IN A BOOK OF STONES
A COLD VOICE IN A ROOM OF IRON CLOCKS
A FROZEN HOOF THAT CLATTERS ON MY BONES.

These factors (pain and death) are essential factors,
geared to the earth's ellipse and the motion of the belly.
Enclosed by a void, enclosing an abyss
I by detesting such essential factors
have set the void to war with the abyss and tear me harder,
I will not be torn.

STILL AN IMPLACABLE VOICE SHRIEKS IN THE SUN,
THESE INSULTS STRIKE AT THE FACE OF THE SUN,
OPPOSE THEM!

Oh do not doubt I know my danger.
Movement engenders friction, blood is struck in the heart,
every awareness implies some sort of collision:
but to fight pain and death with every weapon
would make war total, leave no hope of peace,
I will have peace.

STILL AN IMPLACABLE VOICE SHRIEKS IN THE SUN,
THESE INSULTS STRIKE AT THE FACE OF THE SUN,
OPPOSE THEM!

Is it not right to attempt to be like God?
To gain an equal acceptance of larks and cancer
and to go gentle into that goodnight?
Yes, total acceptance is death for something human
but accepted death is seldom troubled by pain,
I have been man too long.

STILL AN IMPLACABLE VOICE SHRIEKS IN THE SUN,
THESE INSULTS STRIKE AT THE FACE OF THE SUN,
OPPOSE THEM!

Who unpick their anatomy
in ecstasy and agony,
can find a self within no part
of backbone, belly, brain or heart.
Selfhood is the unity.

I tried to know a deity
who justified morality
and found a good god cannot fit
the outer void, the inner pit.
God is the iron grid of law upholding the totality

God is the brightness without edge informing the totality.

That death will break this salt-fresh cockle-hand
is simply wisdom. Horror not, nor pain
poison the sunlight, though they haunt the brain.
The fact casts shadows which have paralysed the will
in error, for these shadows cannot kill.
Fearing becomes reflection
                              rippled in a stream
                                              of thought
                            upon the sand
where death will break this salt-fresh cockle-hand.

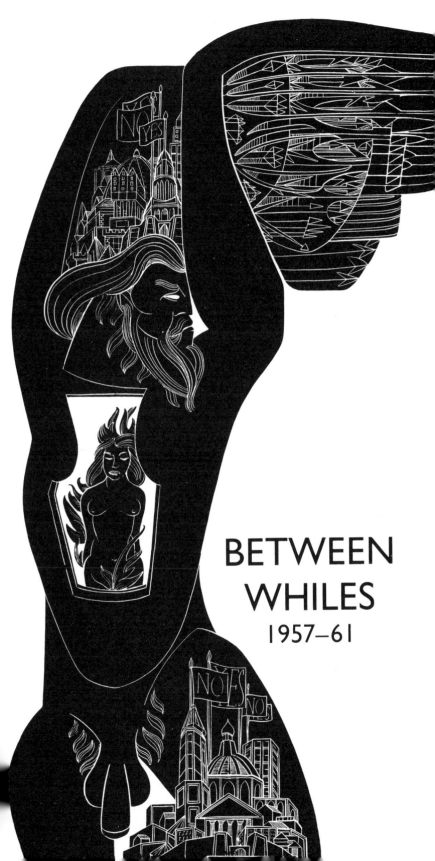

BETWEEN
WHILES
1957–61

Terrible structures have been erected upon the skyline
through which the sun must grin on rising
so that dawn and dusk have become times of tainted light
and only at noon when the rays fall directly on the streets
can we see with clarity.

Condemned to this protection by our law
we cannot wholly loathe imprisonment.
We were born here. Sometimes
I think there is a mystery in dawns and gloamings
a crime has made us unfit to look upon.

Inside the box of bone, the parcel of flesh,
under the helmet of that noble head,
the figure of a naked woman stands,
small, beautiful, obscenely mutilated.

God knows she has achieved many things:
heart, spine, a brain to cap them,
the use of words and fire
till now, enshrined in ribs of dragon armour
all her weapons seem a weary weight,
her wounds not worth protecting.

Because the city was built in time of mutiny
my fingers crumble it down to its foundation.
A wrong wish mixed in the mortar
                              deranges this stone flesh.

The father's strength is essential. In isolation
I got it as contraband and the city festered.
Now his hand is a viaduct joining heart to heart.

I will love strangely no longer. The whore is mine.
Hands that depose a mother instate no virgin.
When a son gets his child on a virgin the child is Satan.

In the logical city the mother is always virgin
but a whore legalizes my seed by taking it into her body
making it another son or whore,
herself a new mother and virgin,
and me Lord and father of myself's own city.

For two or three weeks she walked
                              as if she was protecting something
being a curved box with a seed in it, a life enclosing a life.
Her face looked washed in brine and scrubbed by the wind
but something inside ripened it
and she lay a while on the steps in the sunlight,
                                        nearly a woman
and a few vague thoughts came and went in her head.

"Men are strong like dragons."
"Women, though not weak, are in weak positions."
"I always bent like grass in front of the wind,
                                what good did it do?"
"I still love him."

Sometimes Mandragon hurried past with a casual word
and a keen bitter pleasure stabbed her like a knife
to think she would soon suffer his most dreadful insult;
but suffering also the repose and weariness of fruition
she spread her body on the stone in the sun
and prepared to vomit the debris of something human.

Now she had given birth to a death
and the casket has collapsed inward on its vacancy.

We will all go down into the streets of water
and lose each other among the fluid crystal.
When bodies join their reflections both end
                              but it is common knowledge
that bones and memories lie under the stream
          stirred by the moving water
when the heart is nowhere.

Ach, Carole, my heart aches that its ache for you must end.
Dead regrets have no taste,
under the water is neither sweet nor sour and
your sweet belly will become
only this memory.

He will not occur much to us again
unless in the thin way thoughts occur
who was wild and solid and broke doors in
and had women and clay his hands knew how to touch.

Now what we love in him deprives us of him.
Jokes, height, fox-grin, great irony and nose
will not occur much to us again.
They have been put in a box to rot.

Night air took the heat from his brain
as he lay with cracked head under a wall.
Metal and stones stay shapeless because he is dead.
His clay crumbles. His women mate elsewhere.
He will not occur much to us again.

The stones are lightly held between the roots
of hopeful lives that rise and rock like trees.
Their leaves shake several seasons in the air,
they feel a while the light for which they grow
and then are seasoned bare.

I do not live by hope, but certainty.
I hold stones tight: these are the things I know.
I build a tower of them. I do not grow.
Distrustful of the air through which I go
I rise, back foremost, slowly to the light.

A growing tree contains both rock and sun.
A loving man has made his facts catch fire
while the wise coward shuffles under him
a heap of facts: his tower is never done.
Cowards die clinging to their sullen heap
unheated by the light of their desire.

Most hearts grow by love
or grow by the feel of a loved somebody gone
and the loss gone have nothing to do
but beat and keep a desolate flow of blood.

Strong false hearts, thudding with a phoney love,
not false to life, fulfil some body a while
and the body gone have nothing to do but repent.
It is the weak true hearts that are false to life.

This weak true heart did not satisfy who it loved.
This flesh is blunt. It cannot feel but by loss
and the loss gone, has nothing to do
but sit in a room where dusk and the dust thicken.

Once birdlight and wind in a suburban street
made an absence full of a loved somebody gone
but the loss is gone now. There is nothing to do.
And nothing to do. And nothing to do.

"When wounds did not hurt those who inflicted them
"I was born in a city built over the desolate garden.
"The fall was an obscure event involving grandparents.
"I looked back without loss to an uncushioned womb,"
said Thaw,
rolling the syllables over and under his tongue.

"Logic first made the world my bleak home, showing
"economy under orgy, the use of agony,
"the importance of death, the necessity of dragons,
"and cold a tooth which fitted every wound,"
said Thaw,
rolling the syllables over and under his tongue.

"Though fearful as a child I always dreamed
"of the lovely woman, strong friend, right employer.
"Now I have seen two Beatrices choose murder.
"Friends were responsible. No employer helped,"
said Thaw,
rolling the syllables over and under his tongue.

"And so I came, I and my knotted fist,
"to crack my dreams and suck marrow from them:
"isolated, arrogant, unschooled to receive,
"a leper in armour on a conspicuous height,"
said Thaw,
rolling the syllables over and under his tongue.

"I, who should climb mountains, stand on a rostrum.
"Nobody claps me. The height is not enough.
"I will now go up the side of that common pinnacle
"no one uses for pedestal,nobody knowing the top,"
said Thaw,
still rolling syllables over and under his tongue.

INGE
SØR ENSEN
1961–71

He had wounded himself in the traditional places
but no new crop came from the harrrowed flesh,
and to reject a wound he did not need
would leave the heart unoccupied indeed
if healing only restored the usual surfaces and faces.

Disposed by a quietened will to classical stillness
girls' names no longer evoked the lost erotic chances,
but a wife, a baby, a cat and domestic repose
might flatten the torn ground where feeling grows.
Must everything the heart feels be a sort of illness?

No. Not what the heart feels
                            but what the tongue has declared:
words pour from disease like sweat
                            and breed like germs in a wound.
Love talk, like all talk, is a way of saying no.
We do not explain or complain when sure of the way to go
Meals are exclusive. Famine is always shared.

To enjoy the wife who is his, lovingly, legally
is to be silent. How can he be silent and be?
He imprisons his heart and will not allow a door.
By fearing the gift of love he loves fear more.
It is not fulfilment he wants, but to be wounded regally.

With gravity that holds all possible love
a king and queen go gravely side by side.
His fists are lightly clenched beside his thighs:
she presses his shoulder and she holds his wrist
like a strong mother guiding her son's feet,
like a meek daughter clinging to her guide.

The sculptor only noticed in these two
the things a couple feel when most alone:
the solitude of being me and you —
two feeling hearts in towers of rocking bone.
Not sad to live they advance without fear
to an end they cannot see.

The tide ebbed before flowing strongly,
the moon waned before it seemed a globe,
the sun began setting an hour before noon
and the loved woman was loved wrongly.

There is no excuse for this and can be none.
Soft pricks won't be stiffened by verbal alloy.
But the man resorts to words out of old habit.
The woman has only rage for what she did not enjoy.

I say I will not be
with the brave decent kindly honest men
who merely tolerate the taste of life.
While my wife sleeps
I sit alone at night and drink cheap wine
and stir the source of what is foul in me.

I know that increase cannot come from good.
Thought shows
(by gilding omens of an endless Not
while decent conduct rots us to a ghost)
how complicated desperation is:
or shows the strong dung that feeds my root the most.

Let pain prepare her to sustain my stain,
crush all not me in her brain:
and yet, when semen smells like rotten weed
I wish I were a grain, a stone, a shell
to lie on the ground and be rubbed away
by the decent movements of earth, and air, and rain.

He holds a spoon, certain of what he holds:
nothing more solid-certain than his spoon:
fat clenching fist and hard thing clenched, the same:
no separation between noun and noun.

He waves the spoon, certain of what he waves:
lost in the rhythm of the waving weight
the small face is remote and yet intent:
to feel, think, dream and do are all the same:
no separation between verb and verb.

He drinks his mother: sweetness is a tree
whose branches swing and feed him:
mother, mouth, sweet and drinking are the same:
no separation between noun and verb.

"You shall not" makes him know he is not God,
dividing think from feel and dream from do,
creating adjectives like good and bad,
pronouns like you and me and mine and those,
till home is a place minced into tiny words,
the spoon a perilous thing no longer his
and food the bait of an enormous trap
he hardly will accept as universe.

Looked at from mountain tops and history books
cities spread and flame,
crowds oppose crowds and beget crowds.
Nothing distinguishes man, woman, son or daughter
though sometimes on scaffold or balcony appears
a tiny criminal or legislator
above processions as featureless as the water.

In a room a man sits pondering a debt he cannot pay.
A small boy plays with bricks beside the man's feet.
Nearby a woman mends a shirt, smoking a cigarette.
A clock ticks. A cat sleeps by the fire.
There is noise of brawling from the street.

Crowds thrive and decay on the disastrous horizon.
History forms and breaks like
                              clouds there, repetitive and sublime.
Near at hand disaster is faced, absorbed and passed on
one moment and one life at a time.

I woke to find pain laid on a bare bed with me,
so near, his head, cut in pale stone, was my head,
his brain my brain,
and I could not resign my thoughts to that proximity.
He was so close a company he felt like loneliness.

I tried at length to know a door to make him leave by,
                    a bribe to make him go,
but oh my dear, he grins
from everywhere I look, at everything I do.
I meet his image where I once met you.
He feeds at every meal, beckons down every street
and yet could not withstand
one pressure of your hand.

Come back to me soon. I am changing without you.
My mind turns cold and luminous like a moon.
Keys, coins, receipts accumulate in my pockets.
I grow calm and brutal on beer and thick meat.

"Love is an evil God," the unlovely say.
"She will not warm or kiss or serve us.
"She does not deserve us."
And so they turn to words and wealth and war
and other murderous games which losers play.

The unlovely are special people. They only unite to kill.
They build big pedestals to justify standing apart,
but love is the ardour of a gentle mind.
Lovers give by allowing, and their taking is kind.
It is easy to know the others. We are shrill.

Saying undoes me. Seeing will not let do.
Things numb the hands. Words deafen. Visions blind.
What the mind grasps stuns and deludes the mind.
To say, see, think and feel are all ways
of not having you.

By waiting, not striving, I found the room I wanted.
It was a gift, like life: not bought but rented
from friends made at a stranger's party.
The landlord helped build the long low shelves,
it was cheerful labour. The carpet came from my aunt,
the bay window from a dead architect,
and frames a chestnut tree planted by a neighbour.

But I fear cheerless labour lies behind every gift.
It is sore getting babies out.
Who built this room were badly paid.
Even gifted carpets had a weaver.

By waiting, not striving, I met the woman I wanted.
She stayed a while like air when breathing is easy.
Worst strife was to keep those who liked me least
and kept strife only. My tight grip hurted
them and myself and we parted badly.
This woman moved on like the air,
she unhurt and I undaunted.

But I fear hard breathing is part of every climb,
that the easy grip is cool, the sore grip warm,
that bad partings mean more than kind leavings,
and love cannot last without doing and suffering harm.

TO LYRIC LIGHT
1977–83

Smug Cogito, with flashing spectacles,
shouldered his gun and went to hunt for Sum.
A yapping Ergo led him up the steep
of what he thought were foothills, but were feet
of Sum who sat upon a mountaintop
elbow on knee and hand supporting cheek.
Sum was the mountain's size.
The sun beamed from her eyes.

And all bright summer day Cogito goes
banging at quasis hidden in her skirt,
bawling on Sum to face him like a man.
The noise was a small whimper in her ear
until she closed her eyes, and it was night.
He sheltered in a cave between two toes
and slept. And woke afraid. And crept outside.

Between two dark colossal peaks (her knees)
a starlit, lonely, lovely sleeping face filled all the sky.
At last Cogito
saw he was small, and ignorant, and lame,
and growing in that moment he became
as great as she. She could have been his bride.

He walked away because he did not know.

I am new born.
I want to suck sweet and sing
and eat and laugh and run and
fuck and feel secure and own my own home
and receive the recognition due to a man in my position
and not have nobody to care for me
and not be lonely
and die.

He was, and educated, and became,
residing and remaining and intending,
then on became in, and again,
and later and later again.
He still is, and hopes, and intends,
and may
but is certain to —
one day.

Virgins who touch no body, even their own,
cannot be touched before they are fully grown.
With steady, hungry eyes they long for everyone
till, by long longing,
they can take hold of you by looking.
When hunger is, at length, complete,
it turns anyone into meat
by clever cooking.

But cooks are wicked.
Holding is keeping and keeping locks the door.
I don't want to keep anyone.
I am sick of eating. Give me the pain
that makes me virgin again.

"Not fresh like a flower but fresh like plain new bread,
"as good as God when God will nourish us,
"is what you are," I said
and feared God's goodness, fearing you.
"Love is a far too heavy, precious thing to be my consort.
"Slight her. Cheapen her. Then she may gain my support."

But it is nearly baked.
Light, ground, water, air have life,
life has mind, mind cares, but cares
abused: badly given and taken. Care gladly!
Oh carefulness, inform all I do,
then the good bread can be shared.

Love the friend met in the valley of cunt.
Avoid the enemy made in the valley of cunt.
Dread those who build
civilization badly outside the valley of cunt.

Having wandered far in the amazement of separation
I know that flesh is grass.
Let me graze
in the cleft meadow of Aphrodite.

It is three months since you taught me love can be fun
and one since you came to fruit, breasts weighty and silky.
Now I feel like I seem to you: old, ill-smelling,
a body with whom nothing good can be done.

Untrue, of course. We can join again if
love is more than a noise made in bed.
If not we are both lonely, in pain and afraid
to fruit. Oh trust me. I too can grow.

My fault was, when told the best possible news,
to feel no delight. Allow time.
With time I will show
that when you chose me, you chose right.

I don't sleep well away from you,
don't exercise enough, am morose, am a bore.
Nobody says how well I look any more.
What exercise, what deep sleep you gave!
What delight! What loud exclamations!
I am shocked that this is no longer true,
but loving the delight you unlocked in me
I did not unlock you.
If love had made both of us equally free
it would never have stopped.

The angel said, "His house is burning."
Feeling hot, he awoke.
No smell of smoke, no flame, but all was well.
The room seemed the same, but was not.

He had locked himself into home like a child in a fright.
It felt like jail, himself the governor.
Now, wearing a temporary look,
it warms him and is bright,

burning bright while bright outside
the sun, white clouds and reddening trees burn.
Home is a place we have to leave.
Love it, but don't return.

Who is all fire and wings and hearts and seed?
Has never ended, yet always starts
afresh when the wind changes?
Who gave and changes everything we need?

Who, with all water, weather, ground and spaces,
and many coloured eyes of stone, leaf, star,
won't let us rest in them, but instead
drops dead, stands attentive, raves and races?

Who makes all we joyfully, painfully love march away?
and will one day help us
out in a blink, before we are at last wise,
with a present too suddenly big to hold,
think of, or see, or say?

THE GRAVE COLOURS OF EARTH

BRIGHTEN TOWARD

AN

OPEN BOOK

OF

LIGHT UNSTAINED

BY